WHO IS JESUS?

PROPHET... TEACHER... LIAR... LUNATIC... SON OF GOD

By Maria Tarnev & Tim Wydro

Healthy Living
Ministry

Healthy Living Ministry

Healthy Living Ministry is a holistic health and wellness ministry whose goal is to educate and empower all people to live a productive and wholesome life by following the path of God's perfect design. We want to provide health and wellness information and resources that will allow you to experience a profound impact on your mental, physical, and spiritual well-being. We would love to share our knowledge and 25 years experience about herbal healing, wholesome diet, exercise, prayer and fasting, cleansing and detox, weight loss, and other alternative methods to help with your health concerns. "And God is able to bless you abundantly, so that in all things at all times, having all that you need, you will abound in every good work." 2 Corinthians 9:8...Expect a miracle!

Founders: Maria and Tim Wydro.

Search our website for other books and resources at www. HealthyLivingMinistry.org

This book is dedicated to all those who are searching for a stronger, closer relationship with Jesus Christ.... God Bless, Tim & Maria.

TABLE OF CONTENTS

Part 3: How to Have A Personal Relationship With Jesus

Part 4: Becoming More Like Jesus

INTRODUCTION

Who is Jesus? This simple, controversial question has been a source of debate and discussion for more than two millennia. It is a question that has been addressed not only by theologians and Christian pastors, but also by philosophers, scientists, archaeologists, historians, teachers, and ordinary lay-thinkers.

It also happens to be the single most important question you could ever answer in your own life. In this book we'll discuss not only who Jesus is, but why what you believe about him is of the utmost importance. The Bible teaches that Jesus is the only way to eternal life, the only way to a right relationship with God. If that's not true, then you have nothing to worry about. But what if it is? What if what you believe about Jesus really does determine your eternal destiny?

At the end of each chapter you'll find a few questions for self-reflection, which I would encourage you to seriously consider before moving on to the next portion of the book as they may help you identify what you believe and, by doing so, lead you into a deeper understanding of yourself and God.

My prayer for you is that you would approach this text not as a critic, but with an open mind and heart, and that God would reveal himself to you in a way he never has before. In Jesus' name, Amen.

PART 1

Searching For Truth

Chapter 1

THE QUESTION BEFORE
THE QUESTION

Who are you? Before we try to get to know and understand Jesus—who he is, what he taught, what he did, and why it should matter to you-—I think it is important to first know and understand yourself. "Know thyself" is a well-known aphorism that has been handed down since ancient Greece, yet many of us today still find ourselves searching for who we really are. Students go off to college on a journey of self-discovery with the hopes of finding out not only what they will do for the rest of their lives, but who they will be for the rest of their lives. Men and women spend hours studying self-help books, hoping to find the answer to life's lingering questions, like "Who am I?", "Why am I here?", and "What is the purpose of all of this?"

Many people have turned not just to self-help books but to their own intellect for the answer to these questions. They try to understand themselves through reason or science. Others seek their answers from their own hearts. They believe the best answers come from being in tune with their own feelings, though, if we are honest, what we learn from following reason or feelings alone, leaves us with more questions than answers.

Some of us have tried to find our identity in our careers. Instead of seeking to understand our purpose, we have simply created a purpose for ourselves and made that our identity. We climb corporate ladders, trying to find solace in wealth and success, while in the back of our minds we all know that the towers we are building will one day come toppling down. Money doesn't last forever, neither does prestige. We only have one life to live, and many of us struggle and strain to build an empire (or, at the very least, a hefty bank account), but to what end? To leave it all behind when we die.

Some of us try to find our identity, our purpose, in our families. I am a mom. That is who I am, and who I was made to be. But when your job is done, your sons and daughters move out, and you start to suffer from empty-nesters syndrome, what then? Will you wait by the phone for them to call so you can fulfill your purpose?

We so quickly lose the sense of satisfaction that comes with any of life's earthly endeavors. But why? Why doesn't the goodness we experience stick to our souls, like soul-food sticks to our ribs? Perhaps it is because we were created for more than this earth has to offer.

See, if we truly want to understand ourselves, we must understand where we came from. If we are a product of chance, nothing more than the lingering result of some cosmic explosion that occurred sometime in the distant past, then it is no wonder we are struggling to find our way. I mean, if our roots are based in chance and meaninglessness, why should we expect our lives to be any different? But if we are truly a part of something greater, if we were designed by a Creator, then perhaps we need to look to him to find the answers to our deepest questions.

QUESTIONS FOR SELF-REFLECTION:

What are some things you've tried to find fulfillment and satisfaction in?

Were you satisfied in those things for long?

Can those things satisfy you eternally, or do you long for something better?

Prayer point: Ask God to show you just how unfulfilling and temporary the things of this world can be so that you can better understand the satisfaction only he can provide.

Chapter 2

A PRODUCT OF CHOICE

The Bible, a love-letter of sorts that was inspired by God and written down for the sake of humanity, says we are not a product of chance, but a product of choice. It teaches that there is a loving and almighty God who created all things seen and unseen, including human beings. We are not merely a product of chaos in the cosmos; we were created on purpose, for a purpose. And the only way to discover our purpose and identity is to turn to the one who created us.

Think about it this way: If you look into your kitchen cabinets where you keep your dishes, it quickly becomes apparent that each item you see was designed with a specific purpose in mind. Bowls are better equipped for holding liquid than plates, pitchers have spouts for pouring, saucers have small rings on them to indicate where a teacup is supposed to be placed, and so on—you get the point. The person who created your dishes decided what purpose they would serve, and in doing so gave them an identity.

In the same way, our Creator is the one to whom we must look if we really want to know ourselves, to understand the purpose for which we were created, and to find lasting satisfaction in being who we were created to be. If we fail to look to the source of who we are, and instead spend our whole lives searching for answers in other areas, we will continue to feel the frustration and burden of our unanswered questions.

QUESTIONS FOR SELF-REFLECTION:

Have you ever before considered there might be a higher power?

If so, what do you think he is like and how do you know?

If you could know for sure that there is a Creator, would that change the way you view yourself and your purpose in life?

Prayer point: Ask God to reveal himself to you as you seek answers about him.

Chapter 3

WHAT IS TRUTH?

Finding answers to our deepest questions require us to acknowledge this truth: There is a God. He is the creator and sustainer of all things, but how do we know he exists? The short answer is he has revealed himself to us.

The Bible contains 66 books that were written by 40 different authors from all walks of life, including kings, fishermen, tent-makers, shepherds and priests. The book was written over the course of about 1,500 years, but despite taking so long to come together, and despite being written by so many different people, it is an extraordinarily cohesive book.

But the Bible is more than just a book of facts, it is a recorded history of God's revelation. At different intervals in human history God has made himself known and has intervened in human affairs. He has influenced wars, raised up kings, torn down tyrant nations, and helped the hurting. He has offered wisdom and advice and commands to those who would listen. He has spoken audibly to some, through prophets to others, and to others he has spoken in silent whispers to their hearts.

Why should this matter to you? Because it means God is not distant. He wants to be, and is, involved in the creation of which you are a part. It means God wants to be known, to be found by those who genuinely seek him. I believe what God spoke to the ancient Israelites through the prophet Jeremiah is also true for you. He said, "You will seek me and find me when you seek me with all your heart" (Jeremiah 29:13).

It is also important to recognize that when God revealed himself to humanity he made himself known as the only God. Some of us may come from religious backgrounds which include many deities, but throughout the scriptures God continually rescues his people from the hands of those who worship such "gods."

In today's day and age it is also popular to hold to some sort of vague spirituality, or a belief in some undefined higher power, but God is not undefined, and neither should our faith be. God did not reveal himself in order to be vague. He revealed himself in order to let you know exactly who he is. He is strong, compassionate, loving, faithful, and forgiving. He revealed these characteristics in the past, and he continues to reveal them to us through the Bible and through the continued work of the Holy Spirit on earth.

QUESTIONS FOR SELF-REFLECTION:

Is it important to you to know that God wants to be known? Why?

Does any of the information in this chapter challenge what you previously believed about God?

Prayer point: Ask God to reveal his character to you, so that you might understand the nature of who he truly is.

Chapter 4

REVELATION LEADS TO RIGHT RELATIONSHIP

God has revealed himself to us, and in doing so he has also revealed to us who we truly are, how we came to exist, and why were are here. One of his purposes as revealed in the Bible is that he is trying to restore everything into right relationship with himself. In the ancient past, the Bible teaches, the first humans sinned against God by disobeying him, and ever since then humans have continued sinning and suffering the consequences of their rebellion.

What consequences, you ask? From an earthly perspective, the consequences are as varied as the sins. Greed, selfishness, violence, lust, and injustice have ruined countless lives. Sin has also caused a rift between us and God, so that our souls are not truly alive because they are disconnected from the source of life.

But the good news is God did not abandon us to our own devices despite the fact that we, his creation, rebelled against him. Instead, he devised a plan to restore his creation to a right relationship with him, and Jesus was the key player in that plan (more on that later). God wants to reconnect with humanity. More specifically, he wants to connect with you.

QUESTIONS FOR SELF-REFLECTION:

Do you sense the disconnect between you and God?

What does it say about God that he would reveal himself and enact a plan to save us?

Prayer point: Take a moment to thank God that he has a plan in place that allows you to form a relationship with him.

Chapter 5

YOUR CHOICE

God could demand our allegiance, and in a way he does, but he isn't just forcing us to follow him. Instead, he has chosen to show off his goodness so that we might turn to him with gratitude and joy. He has extended an invitation to all of us, an invitation to enjoy his goodness, to experience who he is. It is up to you whether or not you will accept what he has to offer.

One thing is certain: We all have to make the choice. The Bible is clear that though the human body dies the soul continues on into eternity. It is also clear that those who know and obey God will spend eternity with God in paradise, and those who don't will be eternally separated from God in hell—a place of torment created for Satan, God's nemesis, and his fellow demons. It isn't pleasant to talk about, is it? It is not supposed to be. God wants us to choose a better way.

In 2 Corinthians 7:10, the Apostle Paul, who met Jesus face-to-face only after Jesus had already resurrected from the dead, teaches, "Godly sorrow brings repentance that leads to salvation and leaves no regret, but worldly sorrow brings death." So you see, God allows us to experience temporary discomfort in our souls in order to help us find eternal comfort in him!

This choice you must make is the most important choice of your life, because it will forever affect you beyond the few short years you will live on earth, and you should know that choosing to do nothing is a choice in and of itself. We only have one life, one opportunity to get it right.

Undoubtedly you still have many questions, as you should. I hope this book answers at least some of the big ones. The truth is Christians sometimes come across as people who have all the answers, making those of us who have questions feel insecure, but the truth is God is delighted by our honest search for answers, because he knows real truth always points back to him. In James 1:5 it states, "If any of you lacks wisdom, you should ask God, who gives generously to all without finding fault, and it will be given to you." He is generous with his knowledge and wants our skepticism to lead to him, so don't be afraid to ask him for direction, but you must choose to pursue the truth.

QUESTIONS FOR SELF-REFLECTION:

Would you consider yourself a skeptical person by nature?

Does your skepticism keep you from making choices like this all-important one?

Prayer point: Ask God to help you see through any prejudice and skepticism to the truth of what he has to teach you.

Chapter 6

LOSS AND THE END OF OURSELVES

Questions about who we are, where we are headed, and whether or not God cares about us are never more prevalent than in times of struggle or loss. Tragedy brings out the question we all want the answer to: Is there a purpose for our pain? Is there a reason for our suffering, or is it completely needless? Obviously this answer has the potential to be very complex, but let's try to simplify it a bit. Have you ever heard it said of someone that they "hit rock bottom"? What is interesting about this phrase is it is most commonly used in reference to someone who is now a successful, functioning member of society. Their moment of desperation actually catapulted them to bigger, better things in life. They came to the end of themselves, and there they found a new, better self.

Ravi Zacharias is a world-renowned Christian author, speaker, and apologist. He has given talks at Harvard, Yale, and many other prominent universities, providing answers to many philosophical and biblical questions for both skeptics and believers alike. But there was a time in his life when he had far fewer answers. As a child he was a poor student, and he suffered abuse at the hands of his father. As a troubled teenager he responded to an altar call at a Christian rally in his home nation of India, but a few months later he felt crushed by an overpowering sense of hopelessness, and he decided to end his own life.

"I can't tell you I was going through any psychological turmoil, I just had no hope," Zacharias told Youth For Christ in an interview. "There was no tomorrow to live for, and what was I living for today anyway?" He poisoned himself, but survived.

While Zacharias was still in the hospital, the boy's mother read him a verse from the Bible that changed his life. In the verse, John 14:19, it is recorded that Jesus said, "Because I live, you also shall live." Hearing that verse, and so shortly after his own suicide attempt, caused Zacharias to cry out, "Jesus, if you are who you claim to be, take me out of here. I will leave no stone unturned in my pursuit of truth." Zacharias made it out of the hospital, and from then on his life was forever different.

See, what Zacharias acknowledged in that hospital room was that he had hit his "rock bottom." He came to the end of who he was, but there, at the end of himself, he discovered his true value, his true hope, and his true purpose. The mistake would be to think that coming to the end of yourself is the end, when the truth is coming to the end of yourself—and all the ways you have tried to find hope and fulfillment in this world before—is just the beginning of something better.

Jesus said, "If you cling to your life, you will lose it, and if you let your life go, you will save it" (Luke 17:33). To let go of your life as Jesus described is not to give up on it, but to put it in the hands of one who is greater than yourself. It is to trust your Creator with the outcome of your existence.

Jesus said, "Come to me, all of you who are weary and carry heavy burdens, and I will give you rest. Take my yoke upon you. Let me teach you, because I am humble and gentle at heart, and you will find rest for your souls. For my yoke is easy to bear, and the burden I give you is light" (Matthew 11:28-30). Jesus wants to take the load off your shoulders. Let me introduce you to him.

QUESTIONS FOR SELF-REFLECTION:

Do you think "hitting rock bottom" can actually be beneficial to us? In what way?

Prayer point: Pray that God would help you see your own faults in light of his perfection so that you can truly understand your need for him.

PART 2

Who is Jesus?

Chapter 7

WHAT CONTEXT WAS JESUS BORN INTO?

Jesus was born in the town of Bethlehem (which is located in modern-day Palestine) during a time of great political tension between the many groups who had influence in the region. At that time Israel was under the thumb of the Roman Empire, which invaded the area in the century before Christ's birth. Roman governors were set up over the region, and their responsibilities were to maintain order (Roman soldiers helped maintain the peace and quell any attempted revolts), administer justice, and collect taxes. The tax-collection system was often abused, however, which frustrated the Jews who were forced to submit to it and caused them to despise tax collectors in general.

Another earthly authority Jesus was born under was a ruler named Herod, a king who attempted to kill the infant Jesus shortly after his birth, according to the Book of Luke. He tried to manipulate the wise men, who had travelled from the east to worship the young Jesus, into telling him where the Messiah could be found, but an angel intervened and told them not to disclose where Jesus lived. In response, Herod slaughtered all of the male children age two and younger so the newborn "King of the Jews" would be killed as well, but an angel warned Jesus' parents of the attack in advance so they fled the area, for a time, with their son.

Another group that influenced the politics of the time were the Pharisees, who were a group of Jewish leaders whom the people looked to for decisions and opinions regarding the Jewish law. They also served as the primary human antagonists of Jesus during his ministry, because they saw him as a threat to the honor and authority they had enjoyed for so long. Jesus criticized them for heaping unnecessary and unbiblical religious requirements on the Jewish people, for holding them to an impossible standard of religious duty. He also criticized them for knowing the words of the scriptures without fully understanding them, and for having so much knowledge but having so little love for the God that the scriptures reveal. Ultimately, it was the Pharisees and other religious leaders, working in conjunction with the Romans, who killed Jesus.

At that time in history there was also a group of people known as the Zealots, a group of Jews who wanted to spark a revolution against Rome. They eagerly awaited the appearance of the Messiah, who they believed would be a military leader and warrior whose purpose was to free Israel from the iron grip of its enemies. The Zealots would not have been surprised at Jesus' coming, because they had long been waiting for him to arrive, but they would have been surprised by the way Jesus viewed his own purpose. He did not see himself as a military commander who had come to vanquish the physical enemies of Israel; he viewed himself as a sacrifice who had come to defeat the deadlier spiritual enemies of all of humankind, which leads us into a discussion about the religious culture Jesus was born into.

Jews at that time followed the tenets of the Old Testament Law, which contained rituals, sacrifices, and other commandments which affected almost every aspect of a Jew's life. Under this Law, the Jewish people had to make regular sacrifices to God as a way of dealing with their sins. The sacrifices they offered were symbolic of the grace of God, because instead of paying for their sins with their own deaths, God permitted them to kill an animal instead.

These sacrifices were offered at the Temple, but an ordinary Jewish citizen could not merely offer the sacrifice unassisted. He needed a priest to make the sacrifice for him. Priests served as intermediaries between men and God, making sacrifices and teaching people the way of God's Law. But when Jesus came, one of the things he came to abolish was the need for a middleman in worship. Through his death on the cross, Jesus acted as both priest and offering when he offered his own life for our sins. Because his sacrifice was perfect it was sufficient to cover all of our sins forever, which means we no longer need to offer animal sacrifices (Hebrews 10:18) nor do we need priests to act as middlemen between us and God. But nevertheless, the system of sacrifices as laid out in the Old Testament is all his fellow Jews knew at the time.

In addition to these things, Jesus was also born into a culture that observed a variety of festivals. Not only did these festivals—all seven of which are described in Leviticus chapter 23—honor God, but they also foreshadowed or revealed something about the mission of Christ as well, according to an article on GotQuestions.org (the website for Got Questions Ministries).

The first festival observed was the Passover. The Passover celebration dates back to the times described in the book of Exodus, when the Israelites were slaves in Egypt. God sent supernatural plagues on the land of Egypt as a way of convincing Pharaoh to let the Israelites go free, and the last of these plagues was one in which every firstborn son in every family in Egypt died in the same night.

God commanded each Israelite household to take one lamb or young goat with "no defects" and sacrifice it the night he was to pass through Egypt to kill the firstborn. They were then to smear the blood of the animal on the doorposts of their homes, letting God know to pass over their home and not harm anyone inside. In this way God killed the firstborn of all the Egyptians but spared the firstborn of the Israelites.

Jesus is considered to be the more perfect Passover lamb. His blood, which was smeared on the cross, causes God to pass over those who have faith in Jesus, enabling them to live. We'll talk more about the significance of the Passover later when we discuss the events leading up to Jesus' death.

The Feast of Unleavened Bread followed the Passover and was a remembrance of how quickly the Israelites had to prepare to leave Egypt. They had to leave so quickly that God told them to make bread without yeast, because it wouldn't have time to rise. In the New Testament, yeast is used as a symbol of evil and corruption.

The Feast of the Firstfruits occurred at the beginning of the harvest season, when the Jews would bring the first of their crops of wheat to a priest as an offering to God, thus recognizing their dependence on God and also remembering how God led them out of Egypt and to the Promised Land. Jesus is described as the "firstfuits of those who have fallen asleep" (1 Corinthians 15:20), thus reminding us that his resurrection was just the beginning and that those who believe will be resurrected to be with him one day.

The Feast of Weeks was celebrated after the grain harvest as a way of thanking God for the harvest. It occurred 50 days after the Feast of Firstfruits offering was given, which is why this festival was also known as Pentecost (which means "fiftieth day"). Pentecost was infused with more meaning when, 50 days after the resurrection of Christ, the Holy Spirit showed up to counsel us and guarantee that the promise of salvation would be fulfilled.

The Feast of Trumpets, which took place on the first day of the seventh month of each year, was a day of rest marked by blasting trumpets that signified the end of the agricultural year. The sound of a blasting trumpet is also associated with the announcement of Christ's return, with the resurrection of the dead, and the end times (1 Thessalonians 4:16).

Ten days after the Feast of Trumpets came the Day of Atonement, the one day a year in which the high priest was allowed to enter the Holy of Holies in the Temple of God to make an offering for the sins of all of Israel. The Day of Atonement is also a reflection of what Christ has done in his role as priest, presenting a superior offering to God so that our sins might be covered forever.

The final festival is the Feast of Tabernacles (or the Feast of Booths), a seven-day festival in which the Jews were to live in huts made out of palm branches to remind them of how God made the Israelites live in such temporary housing after he brought them out of Egypt. For those who believe in Jesus, this festival could serve as a reminder that our place in this world is temporary, and that eternal life in the Kingdom of God awaits those who follow Christ.

These are the festivals celebrated by the Jews in Jesus' day, and though they are not observed by Christians today, Jesus' life and promises have only deepened their significance.

QUESTIONS FOR SELF-REFLECTION:

Why do you think it's important to know the historical, cultural, and religious context Jesus was born into?

Are you at all surprised by how much the Old Testament foreshadows the work of God through Jesus?

Prayer point: Ask God to continue to open your eyes to the context Jesus lived in so that the picture of who he is becomes increasingly clear to you.

Chapter 8

THE HISTORICAL JESUS

Many historians recognize the historical existence of Jesus, even if they don't recognize his miracles or the validity of his teachings. The books of the New Testament, many of them being letters or narrative accounts of Jesus' life written by early church leaders and Christ-followers, were being circulated even while eyewitnesses to Jesus' life and teachings were still alive. People at that time did not deny his existence, even if they denied who he claimed to be—the Son of God.

Josephus was a Jewish historian, priest, and aristocrat who aspired to present Judaism as an admirable religion to the Roman rulers, writing at least two of his historical works in Greek, according to an article on the Biblical Archaeology Society's (BAS) website. In one such work, Jewish Antiquities, this non-Christian historian mentions Jesus on two separate occasions. First, Josephus describes James (author of the New Testament book of the same name) as "the brother of Jesus-who-is-called-Messiah." Second, Josephus makes a lengthier reference to Jesus as a "wise man" who "did surprising deeds" and "won over many Jews and many of the Greeks." He also refers to Jesus' execution as being ordered by Roman governor Pontius Pilate (which lines up with the biblical account), and mentions that those who followed Jesus did not give up following him even after his death.

Why are the words of Josephus so important? Because his writings took place just a few decades after Jesus' life on earth. Josephus was born in 37 A.D. and died in 100 A.D., and this closeness in time to the events of Jesus' life, along with the fact that he was a non-Christian making purely historical remarks, make his comments on the historicity of the Christ more reliable.

Another non-Christian historian whose words give strength to the idea that Jesus is an actual, historical figure was Roman historian Tacitus, who was alive at the same time as Josephus (c. 55 A.D. to c. 118 A.D.) and openly hated Christians, according to the same BAS article. In Annals, Tacitus recounted a time Emperor Nero used Christians as scapegoats to remove the suspicion that he had ordered part of Rome to be burned. Tacitus writes, "Therefore, to put down the rumor, Nero substituted as culprits and punished in the most unusual ways those hated for their shameful acts ... whom the crowd called 'Chrestians.' The founder of this name, Christ [Christus in Latin], had been executed in the reign of Tiberius by the procurator Pontius Pilate ... Suppressed for a time, the deadly superstition erupted again not only in Judea, the origin of this evil, but also in the city [Rome], where all things horrible and shameful from everywhere come together and become popular."

So you see, even historians not far removed from the days of Jesus acknowledged his historicity. But one of the things that frustrates some who seek to understand Jesus from a historical perspective is how little archaeological evidence there is of his existence. He never held a political position, and as someone who stood opposed to many of the political forces of his day, he was never recognized with monuments, statues, or other long-lasting evidences of his existence. In fact, because of the resurrection, even his body is nowhere to be found! But just because archaeological evidence is scarce doesn't mean it doesn't exist.

Once such piece of evidence is a first-century ossuary (a box in which bones were placed to be permanently buried after the flesh had entirely decayed) which has these words inscribed on its side in Aramaic, the language spoken by Jesus: "James, son of Joseph, brother of Jesus." While allf three of these names were fairly common during the lifetime of Jesus Christ, an article from the Institute for Creation Research states, what makes this inscription particularly interesting is the fact that it mentions a brother at all. Brothers wouldn't typically be mentioned in these inscriptions unless the brother was truly noteworthy, and the fact that all three names line up with the biblical account of who James was adds authenticity to the idea that the biblical James was buried in the box, and the historical Jesus was truly his brother.

QUESTIONS FOR SELF-REFLECTION:

Does it surprise you to learn there were non-Christian historians who recognized the existence of Jesus?

Prayer point: Ask God to help you see beyond the historical existence of Jesus into the character and nature of who Jesus is.

Chapter 9

JESUS IN THE OLD TESTAMENT

Now that we've established the existence of Jesus as a historical figure, we can start learning more about him. But with Jesus we can't start from the moment of his birth, because thousands of years before he was born people were already talking about him. The Old Testament writings contain prophecies about the coming Messiah, discussing how he would come, his purpose, and more. Jesus fulfilled many of these prophecies.

It was foretold that Jesus would be Jewish, born of a virgin (Isaiah 7:13-14), in the town of Bethlehem (Micah 5:2), as an heir to the throne of King David (Isaiah 9:6-7). He was to be preceded by a messenger who would prepare the way for him (Isaiah 40:3), who we now know as John the Baptist (a man who told the Jewish people to repent and turn to God before Jesus' public ministry began). Jesus was predicted to be a priest "in the order of Melchizedek" (Psalm 110:4), or one who stands alone outside of other priestly family lines, which he showed himself to be when he offered himself as a sacrifice. It was predicted that he would be rejected by his own people (Isaiah 53:1-4), hated for no good reason (Psalm 35:19), treated like a criminal (Isaiah 53:12), and that he would suffer and die for the sins of the world (Isaiah 53:4-6, 10-11).

Not only was his birth and life accurately foretold, but even more incredible is the fact that his resurrection from the dead was also predicted both in the Old Testament (Psalm 16:9-11) and by Jesus himself in the New Testament (Mark 9:31, Luke 9:22). Jesus prophesied about his own death and resurrection before it happened, and his words were recorded that we might believe in him.

The Old Testament prophecies about Jesus tell us much about who he would be as the Messiah. The Messiah is a prophet, priest, and king, three roles which had been largely distinct from each other in the past but which were thoroughly united in Christ. He correctly prophesied about the future, served as a priest in offering himself as a sacrifice, then, after his resurrection, spoke about his role as a king when he stated, "I have been given all authority in heaven and on earth" (Matthew 28:18). He is truly the "King of kings and Lord of lords" (Revelation 19:16).

QUESTIONS FOR SELF-REFLECTION:

Why is it beneficial to understand the prophecies surrounding Jesus?

How do they help you, specifically, better understand who he is?

Prayer point: Thank God that he helped us understand Jesus better by allowing people to prophecy about his person and purpose.

Chapter 10

JESUS AND THE GOSPELS

The Gospels are the first four books of the New Testament—

Matthew, Mark, Luke, and John—which are each an account of the life, miracles, and teachings of Jesus. The word "gospel" is derived from the Greek word euangelion which means "good news," so the four Gospels are the good news about Jesus in narrative form.

Each of the Gospels was penned by a different author to a different audience, and for that reason each narrative highlights different aspects of Jesus' life and ministry, according to an article by Chuck Missler on Khouse.org. The Book of Luke, for example, was written by Luke, a doctor and believer in Jesus, to a dignitary named Theophilus so that Theophilus might believe everything he had been taught about Jesus. Luke writes that he has "carefully investigated everything [about Jesus] from the beginning" (Luke 1:3), and because he tries to provide a thorough account "from the beginning" he gives more detail about the birth of Christ than any of the other authors.

The emphasis throughout the Book of Luke is on Christ's humanity. In Mark, the shortest of the Gospels, the focus is on Christ as an obedient servant to his Father. In Matthew the emphasis is placed on the fulfillment of Old Testament prophecies and on Jesus as the Messiah of the Jews, specifically.

In John, the last of the Gospels, the focus is on Jesus as the Son of God. The book contains seven powerful "I am" statements, or declarations Jesus made about himself to reveal who he is to us. These statements are even more powerful when explained in a Jewish context, because in the Old Testament when Moses asked God what his name is, God responded by saying, "I am" (Exodus 3:14). In essence, each of Jesus' "I am" statements is also a declaration that he is God.

Here is a list of the "I Am" statements:

"I am the bread of life. Whoever comes to me will never be hungry again. Whoever believes in me will never be thirsty" (John 6:35).

"I am the light of the world. If you follow me, you won't have to walk in darkness, because you will have the light that leads to life" (John 8:12).

"I am the gate. Those who come in through me will be saved. They will come and go freely and will find good pastures. The thief's purpose is to steal and kill and destroy. My purpose is to give them a rich and satisfying life" (John 10:9-10).

"I am the true grapevine, and my Father is the gardener. He cuts off every branch of mine that doesn't produce fruit, and he prunes the branches that do bear fruit so they will produce even more" (John 15:1-2).

"I am the good shepherd. The good shepherd sacrifices his life for the sheep" (John 10:11).

"I am the resurrection and the life. Anyone who believes in me will live, even after dying. Everyone who lives in me and believes in me will never ever die" (John 11:25).

"I am the way, the truth, and the life. No one can come to the Father except through me" (John 14:6).

Through these statements Jesus revealed not only his identity as God, but also his purpose in coming to earth. The Book of John is the only Gospel in which they are recorded, because John's audience and emphasis were different from the other Gospels.

Even so, the Gospels do share many similarities. Matthew, Mark, and Luke in particular are called the Synoptic Gospels because they include many of the same stories with similar wording. The opposition of the Jewish religious leaders plays a major part in each of the texts, as does Jesus' death, burial, and resurrection. The crucifixion and resurrection of Jesus are the most foundational tenets of the Christian faith, so it isn't at all surprising that these two pieces are highlighted by all four of the Gospel writers.

All of the Gospels also mention the miracles of Jesus, though only three miracles (the resurrection, the feeding of 5,000 men with a few fish and loaves, and some variation of healing the blind) appear in all four Gospels. Many of Jesus' miracles were healing miracles, which tells us something about the compassionate character of the Christ.

In Matthew chapter eight, for example, a man with leprosy declared, "Lord...if you are willing, you can heal me and make me clean." Jesus responded by saying, "I am willing... Be healed!" Time and time again the Messiah displayed his willingness to provide help for the hurting by healing those who were blind, leprous, paralyzed, and sick. He even raised to life someone who had died (John 11:40-44)!

As a teacher, Jesus distinguished himself from other religious leaders mentioned in the Gospels by the authority with which he spoke. In the first chapter of Mark, Jesus drives a demon out of a man, causing everyone watching to exclaim, "What sort of new teaching is this?...It has such authority! Even evil spirits obey his orders!" (Mark 1:27). Sometimes he taught by simply speaking principles, while at other times he spoke in parables (or short stories that illustrate spiritual truths) so that those who truly listen to his teaching may understand but others may not (Matthew 13:10-12).

Jesus taught on a wide variety of topics during his earthly ministry, often challenging commonly-held beliefs about God and religion, but for the sake of brevity we'll just focus on those topics he addresses in the Sermon on the Mount. In this famous sermon outlined in Matthew, chapters five through seven, Jesus tells his disciples how they are to live on this earth, thus revealing a constitution of sorts for those who belong to the Kingdom of God.

Jesus says his disciples are to do good deeds so everyone will praise God. He argues that sin (especially as it relates to lust and anger) is birthed in the heart long before we act on any such impulses. He teaches about love, and how perfect love requires his followers to not just love those who love them, but to love their enemies as well.

He warns that people who pray or practice generosity publicly, simply for the sake of gaining the attention and approval of other men and women, will receive no additional reward for their prayers or their giving. He warns about treating money like an idol, stating, "No one can serve two masters...You cannot serve God and be enslaved to money" (Matthew 6:24). In this section of the scriptures he also offers what is known as the Golden Rule, "Do to others whatever you would like them to do to you" (Matthew 7:12).

He also teaches on topics like prayer and fasting, judging others, worrying about daily needs, making vows, revenge, the Jewish Law, and more, all just in the Sermon on the Mount! The "I am" statements in John, which point to Jesus as the sole source of salvation, in conjunction with the Sermon on the Mount, which explains how believers should live as members of the Kingdom of God, combine to provide a good overview of Jesus' teachings within the Gospels.

QUESTIONS FOR SELF-REFLECTION:

Why do you think God would allow the story of Christ's life on Earth to be told from several different perspectives?

How do you think having different accounts of Jesus' life can be beneficial to your understanding of who he is?

Prayer point: Ask God to give you faith to begin trusting in the biblical claims about Jesus.

Chapter 11

JESUS OF THE NEW TESTAMENT

The best way to really get to know Jesus is by examining the New Testament, which includes the Gospels, church history (the Book of Acts), the epistles (letters written by followers of Jesus), and prophecy (the Book of Revelation). A thorough examination of the New Testament reveals not only what Jesus did during his time on earth, but also what his followers believed about him after his death and resurrection.

The Gospels are very clear about why Jesus came to Earth. When he was about 30 years old and was ready to start his public ministry, he went to the synagogue in his hometown and read these words from the Old Testament Book of Isaiah:

"The Spirit of the Lord is upon me, for he has anointed me to bring Good News to the poor. He has sent me to proclaim that captives will be released, that the blind will see, that the oppressed will be set free, and that the time of the Lord's favor has come" (Luke 4:18-19).

After reading this, Jesus declared, "The Scripture you've just heard has been fulfilled this very day!" This was Jesus' purpose, not only to physically help people in need, but to help the spiritually poor, captive, blind, and oppressed. Wherever he went, Jesus' prescription to these people was "repent," or turn away from sin, "and believe the good news" (Mark 1:15).

Everything Jesus did was in line with this purpose, and because of this, those who refused to acknowledge their own spiritual shortcomings (namely the Pharisees and religious leaders of the day) became his adversaries. While the Pharisees avoided those who were deemed unclean—tax collectors, prostitutes, etc.—Jesus was known to sit down for meals with a variety of "disreputable sinners" (Matthew 9:10). When criticized for doing so, Jesus declared that he had not come to help those who think they are righteous, but rather those who know they are sinners. The religious leaders made themselves appear godly, Jesus argued, but they lacked the true godliness that cannot be earned and can only be given to mankind by God. This true godliness, Jesus made clear, only comes through a relationship with God and not through some sort of religious ritual.

Contrary to the way some may view Jesus, he was not in any way Stoic or emotionally distant. His passion flowed out of him in the form of love, frustration, anger, and even sorrow. He showed love and compassion toward those who sought him for healing. There were times that he expressed frustration at how little faith his disciples had. He displayed anger when criticizing the teachers of the law, because he felt they had led people away from God. And he expressed sorrow over the people of Jerusalem because they did not turn to God despite the many opportunities the Creator had given them to do so. All of these emotions seem to flow out of a deep love for humanity, and the desire to see us reconciled with our God.

But out of all the words and actions of Jesus, none speaks louder than his crucifixion. It would be a mistake to think Jesus was captured, condemned, and crucified against his will, because based on his prophecies and his quiet reaction to being arrested it is clear he willingly offered himself, knowing his sacrifice was the only way to put an end to sin's reign of terror in our lives. As he stated in John 10:18, "No one can take my life from me. I sacrifice it voluntarily. For I have the authority to lay it down when I want to and also to take it up again. For this is what my Father has commanded."

QUESTIONS FOR SELF-REFLECTION:

What does it tell you about Jesus that he was willing to eat and spend time with "disreputable sinners," instead of spending all his time with religious leaders and those deemed "pure"?

Have you ever thought of Jesus as an emotional being? Does it surprise you that he reacted with deep emotions at times during his ministry?

Prayer point: Thank Jesus for voluntarily dying in order to pay for your sins.

Chapter 12

THE LAST SUPPER

Before Jesus' arrest, trial, and crucifixion came The Last Supper, the last meal Jesus ate with his disciples before his crucifixion and the most symbolically significant meal in history. Before the meal took place, Jesus showed the ultimate display of humility by washing the feet of each of his disciples. In that culture, foot washing was a job for a slave, certainly not the Son of God, but Jesus made himself a servant so that his followers might also humble themselves and serve others.

"I have given you an example to follow," he told his disciples at that time. "Do as I have done to you. I tell you the truth, slaves are not greater than their master. Nor is the messenger more important than the one who sends the message. Now that you know these things, God will bless you for doing them" (John 13:15-17). The Son of God took a low position in this world to win not only our souls but also our affections, and we are called to serve people in the same way.

After the footwashing came the actual meal, which was part of the Jewish celebration known as Passover. Remember, Passover is a festival in remembrance of when God passed over the Israelites on the night he killed all of the firstborn sons in Egypt, and it was the blood of lambs on the doorposts of the Israelite homes that let God know which homes to pass over.

So when Jesus spoke of his own sacrifice during the Passover celebration, knowing he would soon become the sacrificial "lamb" himself, he was pointing to the fact that it is his blood that causes God's wrath to pass over Christ's followers. He made this concept even more clear when he broke a piece of bread and declared to his disciples, "Take it, for this is my body." He then gave them a cup of wine and stated, "This is my blood, which confirms the covenant between God and his people. It is poured out as a sacrifice for many" (Mark 14:22-24). This practice of eating bread and drinking wine (or juice) to commemorate Christ's sacrifice is known today as Communion, and it is still practiced by believers all around.

QUESTIONS FOR SELF-REFLECTION:

How important are a person's last words and actions?

Knowing the words Jesus spoke at The Last Supper were some of his final words to his disciples, do you think this lends them special significance? What about the significance of Jesus' act of footwashing?

Prayer point: Ask God to help you understand the sacrifice of Christ and to form a servant's heart within you.

Chapter 13

THE BETRAYAL, TRIAL, AND CRUCIFIXION

A lthough Jesus willingly offered himself as a sacrifice, the person through whom he was delivered to his executioners was Judas Iscariot. Judas had served as a treasurer of sorts for Jesus' ministry, and he would occasionally steal from the money bag for his own gain (John 12:6). Realizing Jesus' life could be traded for wealth, Judas made a deal with the religious leaders in which he would receive 30 pieces of silver for betraying the Messiah.

One remarkable fact about Judas can actually help us to better understand the character of Jesus: Judas was among those who had his feet washed before the Last Supper. Even though Jesus knew Judas was his enemy (Jesus had previously prophesied that someone would betray him) he still treated Judas with care and compassion.

Later that evening, while Jesus was praying in the Garden of Gethsemane, Judas led a group of armed soldiers to meet him and signaled to the soldiers who they were to arrest by kissing Jesus (a customary greeting at that time). Later, after realizing what he had done, Judas attempted to return the silver to the religious leaders, then went and hanged himself.

The trial of Jesus was a farce, complete with false witnesses and trumped up charges. Each of the Gospels tells of the trial in a slightly different way, but what they make clear is that the political forces of the day (which were all in some way threatened by the person and message of Jesus) all played some role in it. The Jewish leaders pushed hard to condemn Jesus to death, accusing him of blasphemy. They took him to Pontius Pilate, the Roman governor who had the authority to issue a death sentence, and accused Jesus of trying to lead a revolt. Pilate sent Jesus to Herod Antipas, the ruler of Galilee, to be dealt with, but Herod sent him back and, despite finding no truth in the Jewish leaders' accusations, Pilate eventually bowed to the pressure and agreed to have Jesus crucified.

Prior to the crucifixion, Jesus was mocked, punched, whipped, spat on, and was forced to wear a crown of thorns. He then carried his own cross to the place of his execution, a hill known as Golgotha (or "the skull"). There, nails were driven into his hands (or wrists) and feet, and the cross was set upright, causing Jesus excruciating pain.

While on the cross, some people mocked Jesus, saying, "He saved others...but he can't save himself! So he is the King of Israel, is he? Let him come down from the cross right now, and we will believe in him!" (Matthew 27:42). Yet Jesus didn't take the bait. Why? Because he chose to save our lives, not his own. It was his sacrifice that gave us the opportunity to believe and be free from the power of sin and death.

QUESTIONS FOR SELF-REFLECTION:

Have you ever been falsely accused of something? How did it make you feel?

What does it say to you about the character of Jesus that he would endure so much pain and suffering for us?

Prayer point: Thank God that his Son would endure the shame and suffering we deserve because of his great love for us.

Chapter 14

THE CROSS

Jesus was killed by way of crucifixion, a form of execution used by the Roman Empire that caused those being crucified to die of asphyxiation as they were crushed by their own body weight while hanging on the cross. It was a brutal way to die, yet today the cross is not a symbol of death, but of hope, because of Jesus' sacrifice.

The cross acted as a sort of altar for this great sacrifice, where Jesus, the Lamb of God, was killed. And he was no ordinary lamb, but rather the "sinless, spotless Lamb of God" (1 Peter 1:19), who was without sin yet died so that sinners could be made righteous. An imperfect sacrifice would not have been sufficient to quench God's wrath, but the sinless Messiah was able to carry the weight of our sin on his shoulders.

At the cross, God "canceled the record of the charges against us" (Colossians 2:14). He freed us from the "curse" that affects all humanity (Galatians 3:13), and became wounded so we might be healed (1 Peter 2:24). In other words, Jesus' hurt equals your healing, if you believe in him. Some people view this message of the cross as foolish, but "we who are being saved know it is the very power of God" (1 Corinthians 1:18).

In the light of the cross, we see not only Jesus but also ourselves as we truly are. We see the contrast between the one who embodied perfection and we who are sinners. We see the punishment that we deserve being poured out on a loving God who deserved none of it. We see the extent to which God is willing to go in order to restore the relationship he once had with mankind. In the cross we see pure, undefiled love.

Jesus said, "There is no greater love than to lay down one's life for one's friends" (John 15:13). In light of the cross we realize we no longer have to stay enemies of God, but we can now live as his friends. We can be made new, and all that God requires is that we receive the gift of God's grace which he made available to us through the cross. For our salvation, all God asks of us is that we put our faith in Jesus.

QUESTIONS FOR SELF-REFLECTION:

Does it surprise you that simple belief is all it takes for you to receive salvation?

How does it make you feel to know that Christ paid the penalty you deserve for your sins?

Prayer point: Ask God to help you understand the cost of your own sin, as well as how he has made salvation free to all of us through Jesus.

Chapter 15

THE RESURRECTION

After Jesus' death, the Gospels say, a wealthy follower of Christ named Joseph of Arimathea got permission from Pilate to take Jesus' body. He wrapped it in linens and had it placed in a new tomb that had been carved out of rock, then he had a heavy stone rolled in front of the tomb to cover it.

The Pharisees remembered Jesus' claim that he would rise from the dead after three days, and feared that one of the disciples would come and steal Jesus' body to make the miracle appear true, so with the help of Pilate they sealed the tomb and posted guards to protect it.

But three days later, just as Jesus had predicted, the tomb was empty and the risen Savior began appearing to people! He wasn't just a spirit or ghost, either. He came back alive in the flesh, and proved it to his disciples by eating with them and by allowing Thomas, a disciple who couldn't believe Jesus had resurrected from the dead, to put his fingers in the wounds given to Jesus during his execution.

According to the Apostle Paul, the resurrected Christ didn't appear only to a few people in a few isolated incidents, either. In 1 Corinthians, Paul states that after Jesus appeared to his Apostles he "was seen by more than 500 of his followers at one time, most of whom are still alive" (1 Corinthians 15:6).

Practically speaking, the good news about Jesus' resurrection is that it was not the last resurrection. Those who believe in him will one day experience a resurrection of their own, and will live again. As I previously mentioned, Jesus said, "I am the resurrection and the life. Anyone who believes in me will live, even after dying" (John 11:25) What I did not elaborate on, however, was the fact that shortly after speaking those words Jesus actually raised a dead man, Lazarus, to life. By believing in Jesus the same power that raised Lazarus from the dead also lives in us and will one day result in our resurrection as well, if we die before Christ returns.

It is important to remember, as was previously stated, that Jesus' resurrection was predicted long before it actually occurred. It wasn't a surprise, or at least it shouldn't have been. King David wrote of the Christ, "For you will not leave my soul among the dead / or allow your holy one to rot in the grave" (Psalm 16:10). Even before his arrest, Jesus also accurately predicted the following: "The Son of Man must suffer many terrible things...He will be rejected by the elders, the leading priests, and the teachers of religious law. He will be killed, but on the third day he will be raised from the dead" (Luke 9:22).

The resurrection was the most significant event in history. If the cross was a moment of terrible sorrow, the resurrection was one of inexplicable joy, because it means we can now join Jesus in life even after death.

QUESTIONS FOR SELF-REFLECTION:

How would your life change if you really believed in a life after death?

Prayer point: Ask God to help you find your hope in the resurrection of Jesus, rather than in the things of this world that are gradually fading away.

Chapter 16

JESUS, THE SON OF GOD

Jesus is unique among other gods and religious leaders because he claims to be both fully human and fully God. He was born to a virgin mother without an earthly biological father, and his true Father is God, who is spirit. At Jesus' baptism (Matthew 3:17) and during his transfiguration (Matthew 17:5) God the Father spoke audibly from heaven and declared Jesus to be his son. In the scriptures Jesus is alternatively called either the "Son of Man" or the "Son of God," reflecting the dichotomy between his physical and spiritual nature.

But is Jesus actually God? Some have tried to argue that just because Jesus is the Son of God doesn't actually make him God. These people claim Jesus never actually stated he was God, when he actually did make such a claim several times and in several different ways.

In Luke chapter five, a group of men brought their paralyzed friend to Jesus to be healed. When Jesus saw their faith he declared to the paralyzed man, "Young man, your sins are forgiven!" This infuriates the Pharisees and teachers who were watching nearby, and they said to themselves, "Who does he think he is? That's blasphemy! Only God can forgive sins!" Jesus' response? He healed the man of his paralysis, thus showing he has the authority as God to heal both the body and soul.

In John chapter 10, some people came to Jesus and asked him to tell them plainly whether or not he is the Messiah. Jesus responds by saying, simply, "The Father and I are one." At this the people pick up rocks and prepare to stone him to death, and when he asks them why they want to kill him they say it's because "You, a mere man, claim to be God."

There are other examples of Jesus claiming to be God in the New Testament, but let's look at an example from the Old Testament as well. We've already established that Jesus' coming was prophesied long before his birth, and about 700 years before Christ was born the prophet Isaiah also declared that the Christ would be God. Isaiah said:

"For a child is born to us, a son is given to us. The government will rest on his shoulders. And he will be called: Wonderful Counselor, Mighty God, Everlasting Father, Prince of Peace" (Isaiah 9:6, emphasis mine).

Jesus is unique among the world's religious leaders because he claimed to be God, but another thing that makes him unique is his resurrection. Many religious leaders have been born, lived, and died, but only one has returned to life after his death, and that is Jesus. The Bible teaches that the resurrected Christ is "the firstfruits of those who have fallen asleep" (1 Corinthians 15:20). This verse is not referring to literal sleep but to physical death, and in describing Jesus as the "firstfruits" this verse indicates that his resurrection was only the beginning. Because Jesus was raised from death, we know that those who love and trust him will also eventually be raised to life. As Paul writes, "For since death came through a man, the resurrection of the dead comes also through a man. For as in Adam all die, so in Christ all will be made alive. But each in turn: Christ, the firstfruits; then, when he comes, those who belong to him" (1 Corinthians 15:21-23).

The question remains: How do we obtain this resurrection? The resurrection is not an accomplishment to be achieved, but rather is a gift that must be received. The scriptures teach that we have all sinned against God, and unless our sins are atoned for we will be punished severely for them. To atone for our sins means to make reparations for them, but we had no way of doing so until Jesus came along! No number of good deeds can cancel out our sin, but Jesus' sacrifice was great enough to pay for them in full. He took our punishment for us so that we might have life.

QUESTIONS FOR SELF-REFLECTION:

How do you view Jesus? Was he just a man? Is he the Son of God, but not God? Or is he actually God in the flesh?

Prayer point: Pray that God would help you see the truth about Jesus' identity.

Chapter 17

THE TRUE SALVATION

What does it mean to be saved? It means your sins are forgiven, you have been brought into right relationship with God, and your eternal destination has been shifted from hell, a place of eternal punishment, to heaven, a place of eternal bliss. As I've already stated, the way we receive this salvation is simple. In Romans, Paul says the following is the message he preached everywhere he went: "If you openly declare that Jesus is Lord and believe in your heart that God raised him from the dead, you will be saved. For it is by believing in your heart that you are made right with God, and it is by openly declaring your faith that you are saved" (Romans 10:9-10). It seems so counter-intuitive, like we should have to work harder to receive salvation, yet we are not saved by our own works but rather by the work Jesus accomplished through his death on the cross.

Once saved, we are called to live for God. We don't return to selfish ways, but rather follow in Jesus' footsteps to become like him, bringing as much glory to God as possible. As Paul wrote, "My old self has been crucified with Christ. It is no longer I who live, but Christ lives in me. So I live in this earthly body by trusting in the Son of God, who loved me and gave himself for me" (Galatians 2:20). So while we cannot be saved by good deeds, we have been made new in Jesus "so we can do the good things he planned for us long ago" (Ephesians 2:10).

The good news is we aren't left alone to figure out how to live for God, because God has sent the Holy Spirit to serve as a counselor to those who believe. The Bible teaches that God sent the Son to die for us, and after Christ's resurrection and ascension into heaven he sent the Holy Spirit to help and advise us. The Holy Spirit does a number of things, including giving believers an assurance of their salvation. Ephesians 1:13-14 declares that "when you believed in Christ, he identified you as his own by giving you the Holy Spirit, whom he promised long ago. The Spirit is God's guarantee that he will give us the inheritance he promised and that he has purchased us to be his own people. He did this so we would praise and glorify him."

Remember, Jesus came to give us a "rich and satisfying life" (John 10:10), but it is a life that you must choose to receive. The difficult work is done, Christ is victorious over death, and now he simply invites you to join him in victory. He invites you to let go of your sin, to turn from your sinful ways and toward God. He invites you to turn toward heaven, toward life. Forgiveness is not something all of us will seek, but it is certainly something we all need.

So if you're ready to give to put your faith in him (to trust him as Savior) and to submit your life to him (to trust him as Lord), then I want to invite you to pray to him by saying the following: "Lord, I realize I'm a sinner. I'm sorry for the wicked things I've thought and done. I realize now that Jesus is God, that he died for my sins, that he rose from death, and I ask that you would forgive me. Help me to love you and serve you well with the rest of my life, until the day we meet each other face to face. In Jesus' name, amen."

If you just prayed that prayer, and in your heart you believe what you prayed, you are now saved! You are no longer an enemy of God; you belong to God. The record of your sins has been destroyed, you are washed clean by the blood of the Lamb, and you are now a new person! Your soul can now be at peace, because your greatest enemies—Satan, sin, and death—can no longer do you harm. Your eternity is secure in God, and starting today he wants to show you how to live to the fullest.

QUESTIONS FOR SELF-REFLECTION:

Did you pray that prayer? How did it make you feel?

If not, why not? What roadblocks are preventing you from receiving your salvation?

Prayer point: If you didn't pray for salvation, ask God to convince you of your need for Jesus.

PART 3

~

How to Have A Personal Relationship With Jesus

Chapter 18

SEEING YOURSELF THROUGH
THE EYES OF GOD

God sees and understands every angle of every situation. He saw the universe when it was created, and he foresees the future with complete clarity. "As the heavens are higher than the earth," Isaiah 55:9 says, so are God's ways are higher than our ways and his thoughts higher than our thoughts. God's perspective is totally unique, and part of developing a good relationship with him is being able to see yourself through his eyes.

God doesn't just see what you have already done, he also sees your potential, who you can become. You were created in his image, and so he sees you as inherently valuable even when you feel worthless. Jesus' death on the cross was God's greatest expression of love, and you must always remember that you are the object of his love. A good relationship with God is perpetually strengthened by the idea that he genuinely loves you and wants you to succeed.

In the Old Testament, Moses tells the people of Israel that God "will never leave you nor forsake you" (Deuteronomy 31:6). God is completely committed to you, and wants you to know that he will not fail you. He is faithful, and even in the lonely moments of your life he wants you to know that you're not alone. Even in the moments that seem bleak or hopeless he wants you to remember he will not fail you. Things might not always go your way, but you can trust that if they don't, he has something better planned for you.

Throughout the scriptures this idea that God is always with his people is reiterated many times. Even Jesus told his disciples "I will be with you always" before he ascended into heaven (Matthew 28:20). What is important to note is that each of these reminders of God's constant presence are accompanied by a call for us to not be afraid. In fact, it is because God is with us that we can live free from fear. His love for us is so deep and his power so strong that though our lives may take unpleasant turns at times, we can be confident he will eventually lead us to a place of rest and that he can provide us with and joy in the meantime.

As our relationship with God develops, it's also important to remember that he wants both his person and plan (at least in general) to be known by us. God's way of doing things may seem foreign or confusing at times, which can frustrate us if we feel like he's being unclear, but we must remember it was God who revealed himself to us, not the other way around. By revealing himself throughout history and by giving us the Bible as a testimony to his person and plan, God has made it clear he wants to be known. So be patient when seeking him, and trust that you will find God when you seek him with all your heart (Jeremiah 29:13).

QUESTIONS FOR SELF-REFLECTION:

Have you ever thought of God as distant? How did this chapter change your perspective of him?

Why do you think it's difficult for humans to see their lives from God's perspective? How would our lives change if we did?

Prayer point: Ask God to help you see yourself through his eyes, that you would understand the love he has for you.

Chapter 19

PRAYER

God speaks to us in many ways—through the Bible, through other people, through life situations, etc.—but in order to have a healthy relationship with him we must speak to him as well. That's what prayer is: an ongoing conversation with God. It is a chance to respond to what he's done so far in our lives and to seek his direction for the future. It is a chance to unburden ourselves with the weight of life's stresses by placing them in the hands of someone much greater than ourselves. It is an opportunity to connect with the Creator, to recharge our spiritual batteries, and gain a fresh perspective on our lives.

Prayer is not just talking to the air, nor is it some sort of meaningless religious discipline, it is bending the ear of God. It is plugging into the greatest power source ever known. James 5:16 says, "The prayer of a righteous person is powerful and effective." In prayer we can ask for provision, protection, and transformation. Sometimes, as a result of prayer, God will completely change our situation, while other times he will give us the strength to endure our situation, but regardless of how he helps us, what is important is that we invite him into our everyday lives.

In prayer we have an opportunity to seek not only strength, but also wisdom. God is not only the greatest source of power but also the greatest source of knowledge and understanding. James says God is "generous" with his wisdom and will provide it to those who seek him (James 1:5).

Prayer is also an opportunity to thank God for everything he's done. In any other relationship it would be ridiculous to continually ask for things and never thank the person providing them, and in the same way we should always remember to thank God in our prayers. Philippians 4:6-7 states, "Don't worry about anything; instead, pray about everything. Tell God what you need, and thank him for all he has done. Then you will experience God's peace, which exceeds anything we can understand." Prayer is the path to peace, so let God know what you need and thank him for what he has done.

But how should you pray? Jesus taught his disciples what has come to be known as "The Lord's Prayer" to give them a pattern, or template, for their prayers. The Lord's Prayer (as found in Matthew 6:9-13) is as follows (with my notes in brackets):

"Our Father in heaven, [who we pray to]

hallowed be your name, [respecting the holiness of God's name]

your kingdom come,

your will be done, [we are seeking God's will, not our own]

on earth as it is in heaven.

Give us today our daily bread [ask for provision].

And forgive us our debts [ask for forgiveness],

as we also have forgiven our debtors.

And lead us not into temptation,

but deliver us from the evil one [ask for protection from our spiritual enemies]."

In addition to The Lord's Prayer, the Bible offers other insights into how we should communicate with God. Jesus says our prayers should be sincere, not for show (Matthew 6:5), and there's no indication that we need to use some sort of special prayer lingo to talk to God. We should be reverent, to be sure, but we should still speak plainly to him.

We should also pray continually. We should pray in our homes, in our cars, at our jobs, and with our friends. We should pray out loud at times and silently at others. There are many ways to pray, but we should take the advice of 1 Thessalonians 5:17 and "Never stop praying."

QUESTIONS FOR SELF-REFLECTION:

What is something you're grateful for?

What is something you're struggling with?

Prayer point: Take a moment to thank God, as well as to ask him for help, based on your answers to the above questions.

Chapter 20

YOUR MINISTRY

You might think it is too soon to discuss how you can minister to others, probably because you don't yet feel qualified to share your faith, but many of the believers in the New Testament wasted no time in sharing their faith in Christ after they first believed. The woman at the well in John chapter four, for example, shared her faith by telling all the people in her town about her encounter with Jesus, which led to many of them to believe in him too. The simple truth is God has called us to share him with the world, and because time is getting short we should not hesitate to begin ministering to others.

One of the best places to start ministering is within the church, because it is there that believers can bring their unique gifts, talents, and perspectives to encourage each other and serve those who don't yet believe. "God has given each of you a gift from his great variety of spiritual gifts," the scriptures say in 1 Peter 4:10. "Use them well to serve one another." The church as a whole is the body of Christ, and we are to use our collective gifts to help one another and show Jesus to the world. So don't be a lone wolf: become a part of a church body where you can receive encouragement and use your gifts to encourage others.

Before Jesus ascended into heaven he left his closest followers with a major task, which has become known as The Great Commission: "Therefore go and make disciples of all nations, baptizing them in the name of the Father and of the Son and of the Holy Spirit, and teaching them to obey everything I have commanded you" (Matthew 28:19-20). Having been disciples themselves, Jesus was now calling them to go out and make more disciples, more followers. We have been called to do the same in our lives.

As you grow and mature in the faith, you should seek to help others (especially those who are younger in the faith) learn to follow Jesus well—this is discipleship. Disciples are more than students, they are people who follow their leader closely, not only so they can listen to their teachings, but also so they can imitate their way of life. Even as you follow Jesus and learn from others in the church, you should seek to connect with younger believers and set the example for them, showing them the way to live for Christ.

But before a person becomes a disciple, he must accept the gospel message for himself. How can he follow Jesus if he doesn't believe in him? And in order for anyone to believe, someone must bring the good news to them. Romans 10:14 says, "But how can they call on him to save them unless they believe in him? And how can they believe in him if they have never heard about him? And how can they hear about him unless someone tells them?"

Let me be clear: Evangelism is every believer's responsibility. Some Christians want to leave Gospel-sharing to the "professionals"—pastors, religious teachers, and the like—but the woman at the well made a huge impact on her town as a result of sharing her own experience with Jesus! So the pastor's job is not to do all the Gospel-sharing himself, but rather to equip the believers under his leadership to minister to others (Ephesians 4:12).

It is important for each of us to share our faith, but just because that's true doesn't mean we inherently know how to do so. There are two major approaches to sharing one's faith: the "come and see" approach and the "go and tell" approach. Philip used the "come and see" approach on his brother Nathanael in John chapter one. Instead of sharing all about Jesus, Philip simply invited Nathanael to come and meet Jesus himself. The modern equivalent of this sort of approach is inviting someone to attend church with you.

The next approach, "go and tell," is where you go to your friends, family, and neighbors and share your faith with them. This usually starts with you sharing how God has impacted your life, then you can follow it up by inviting your listeners to also accept Jesus into their lives by telling them about Christ sacrificing himself for their sins. The Gospel may be an extravagant story, but the Holy Spirit can use even a simple telling of it to change someone's heart.

It is important to note that we are to not only share our faith with unbelievers, but with believers as well. As Christians, we are called to "encourage each other and build each other up" (1 Thessalonians 5:11) as well as to speak "with psalms, hymns, and songs from the Spirit" (Ephesians 5:19). It is our unity in Christ that makes us collectively strong, so don't be afraid to speak up in order to encourage your brothers and sisters in the faith.

Another important component of your ministry is prayer. In 1 Timothy 2:1, Paul instructs his young mentee with the following words: "I urge you, first of all, to pray for all people. Ask God to help them; intercede on their behalf, and give thanks for them." Many people turn to prayer as the last resort, a final attempt at solving their otherwise unsolvable problems, but the Bible suggests it should actually be the first strike, and not just against our own problems either.

Praying for others is powerful, not only because God responds powerfully when we intercede for others, but also because it helps us keep our lives in perspective. How can a man who concerns himself primarily with others really be selfish? When we pray for others, we are inviting God into their situations, whether they know it or not. God can influence people we've never even met, so prayer, in that sense, is like a long-distance spiritual weapon that cannot be defended against by physical or geographic limitations.

One type of prayer Christians often pray over each other is a prayer for healing. Jesus spent a lot of time during his earthly ministry healing the lame, leprous, and blind, and we should still pray for healing today. The Book of James says those who are sick should come to the elders of the church, who will lay their hands on the sick person to pray for them, anointing them with oil, "And the prayer offered in faith will restore the one who is sick" (James 5:15). Though modern medicine is in many ways a blessing from God, we should also seek healing from the Lord. There are some sicknesses only he can heal, and some chains only he can break.

QUESTIONS FOR SELF-REFLECTION:

What gifts or talents has God given you that you could use to encourage and reach others for Christ?

Who can you pray for today that is in need of some extra help in their lives?

Prayer point: Ask God to help someone you know who is in need.

Chapter 21

FIGHTING SPIRITUAL BATTLES

Life is more than just a series of obstacles to get over, it is a series of battles to be fought. The scriptures say we have a real enemy, Satan, who "prowls around like a roaring lion, looking for someone to devour" (1 Peter 5:8). They also say his primary mission is to "steal, kill, and destroy" (John 10:10). He hates God and those who trust in him, so we must always be on our guard. We cannot afford to simply ignore him, or treat him like he doesn't exist, because to ignore our enemy's advances is to open ourselves up to defeat. As John Eldredge says in Wild at Heart, "You can't fight a battle you don't think exists."

Not only do we need to acknowledge that we are in the middle of a fight, but we also need to recognize the nature of this battle is unlike any we have ever faced before. Ephesians 6:12 reminds us that "we are not fighting against flesh-and-blood enemies, but against evil rulers and authorities of the unseen world, against mighty powers in this dark world, and against evil spirits in the heavenly places." If this seems dramatic, that's because it is! There is a lot of fighting going on around us, and if we are going to win the battle we need to be equipped to fight back.

Since the battle is taking place in the spiritual realm, the weapons that will help us overcome our enemies are also spiritual weapons. The Bible talks about putting on "God's armor," which includes "the belt of truth," "the body armor of God's righteousness," shoes made of "the peace that comes from the Good News," "the shield of faith," the helmet of salvation, and "the sword of the Spirit, which is the word of God" (Ephesians 6:13-17). These spiritual weapons protect us from and help us gain victory over our greatest enemies.

In spiritual warfare, it is important to not only have the right tools, but to also have a good understanding of who the enemy is and how he plans to attack. Genesis 3:1 says the serpent (who we know as Satan) was "was the shrewdest of all the wild animals the Lord God had made." He doesn't just attack with force, but with cunning as well. He uses our own weaknesses against us, so instead of trying to convince us to commit sins randomly he tempts us with the thing our flesh wants the most. "Temptation comes from our own desires, which entice us and drag us away," James 1:14-15 says. "These desires give birth to sinful actions. And when sin is allowed to grow, it gives birth to death."

So if Satan tries to manipulate us using the worldly desires within us, then our best defense against him is to guard our hearts carefully. Proverbs 4:23 says, "Guard your heart above all else, / for it determines the course of your life." Imagine being the guard in charge of protecting the gate of a walled city, the city of your heart. Your responsibility is to keep watch and be aware of both who is coming into your city and who is going out. If an enemy approaches, you should close the city gates, not welcome him in! If he gets in he could ravage the town, and Satan's work doesn't often appear to be that of a big, scary villain. He "disguises himself as an angel of light" (2 Corinthians 11:14), appealing to you in an attempt to get you to let him in, but if you arm yourself with the armor of God you will not only be able to recognize him, but you will be able to defeat him too.

In the midst of all of life's battles, with all of the struggles we face on a daily basis, what is, perhaps, most important to remember is the fact that our success is tied directly to the success of Jesus Christ. Colossians 2:14-15 states, "[Jesus] canceled the record of the charges against us and took it away by nailing it to the cross. In this way, he disarmed the spiritual rulers and authorities. He shamed them publicly by his victory over them on the cross." Because Jesus has victory, we too will ultimately experience victory if we remain in him.

QUESTIONS FOR SELF-REFLECTION:

Which temptations are most enticing for you?

How do you deal with it when you're feeling tempted?

How does it make you feel knowing there are outside forces that want to cause you to fail? How does it affect your view of God?

Prayer point: Ask God to equip you for battles against your spiritual enemies, and ask him for the strength, courage, faith, and love needed to endure.

PART 4

Becoming More
Like Jesus

Chapter 22

DAILY HABITS FOR BELIEVERS

We are not just called to follow Jesus, we are called to be like him. He not only taught us how to live, but he set the example for us as well. Paul writes in Ephesians 5:1-2, "Imitate God, therefore, in everything you do, because you are his dear children. Live a life filled with love, following the example of Christ. He loved us and offered himself as a sacrifice for us, a pleasing aroma to God." Christ has shown us through the scriptures what he expects of his followers, but if we're honest it can sometimes feel overwhelming trying to get it right. Perhaps the best way to start becoming like him is to simply get into the habit of getting into his presence every day. Habits are powerful. Philosopher Will Durant once wrote, "We are what we repeatedly do. Excellence, then, is not an act, but a habit." A single prayer, for example, can be powerful, but what is even better is a consistent prayer life. A single reading of the scriptures can be transforming, but even more so is a consistent pattern of engaging with the Word of God.

Jesus said, "If any of you wants to be my follower, you must turn from your selfish ways, take up your cross daily, and follow me" (Luke 9:23, emphasis mine). We need to treat every day like an opportunity to build on the faith Jesus has founded within us, to become better and more like Christ. A great way to do this is to make time to get alone with God each and every day.

Though experiencing life with a community of believers is important to a person's faith, it is also vital that Christians spend time alone with God. Even Jesus "often withdrew to lonely places and prayed" (Luke 5:16). When we spend time alone with God and we truly seek to connect with him, often we come out of that time with a renewed sense of purpose, passion, perspective, and direction.

After pouring ourselves out and spending our energy on the demands of daily life, this quiet time with God is an opportunity to let him pour into us. That's why many believers advise spending this time with God first thing in the morning, because it is a great way to prepare for the day. Find a quiet place where you can pour your heart out to God uninterrupted, and don't forget to take time to thank him for everything he has done for you. If you thank God for the blessings he's given you before you ask for anything, it might help to remind you that your needs are small compared to what God has already provided.

When you pray, make sure you're not just speaking, but listening, too. Be sensitive to the fact that God might have something to teach you during your quiet time, then invite him to speak into your life. Let him know you're receptive to his guidance and wisdom, and that you're hungry to hear from him. Remember, your goal during this quiet time is not merely to get the words of your prayer out into the open, but to really connect with your Creator. Make connecting with God a habit, and there's no telling how he might bless you!

Prayer is key, but in our journey to become more like Christ we must remember to also make a daily habit of reading the Bible. How can we become like Christ if we don't know what he's like? God has much to teach us through the scriptures. Hebrews says God's word is "alive and powerful" (4:12), and 2 Timothy 3:16-17 says, "All Scripture is inspired by God and is useful to teach us what is true and to make us realize what is wrong in our lives. It corrects us when we are wrong and teaches us to do what is right. God uses it to prepare and equip his people to do every good work."

Should we ignore such a powerful, useful resource? The Bible offers answers to so many of our questions, and it is a source of encouragement and hope to those in need. We should crave it more than we crave food, because as Jesus says, "People do not live by bread alone, but by every word that comes from the mouth of God" (Matthew 4:4).

So follow Jesus daily. Seek him in everything you do. Let him, through your consistent encounters with him and his Word, transform your life from the inside out. The Christian life is a race of endurance, one that is filled with both blessings and difficulties, but those who finish it are guaranteed an unfathomably wonderful eternity thereafter. Remember these encouraging and motivating words from Paul in his letter to the Philippians: "And I am certain that God, who began the good work within you, will continue his work until it is finally finished on the day when Christ Jesus returns" (Philippians 1:6).

QUESTIONS FOR SELF-REFLECTION:

What do you need to do to develop these habits in your daily life?

How can you make room in your schedule to accommodate these new habits?

How do you think practicing these things will affect other areas of your life?

Prayer point: Ask God to help you develop new habits that honor him.

REFERENCES

Translations of The Holy Bible used: New Living Translation (2015, Tyndale House Publishers) and New International Version (2011, Biblica Inc.)

(2014, October 21). Ravi Zacharias Tells His Life Story Including His Conversion In YFC. Retrieved from http://www.yfc.net/about/storiesblog/ravi-zacharias-tells-his-life-story-including-his-conversion-in-yfc

Durant, Will. (1926). The Story of Philosophy: the Lives and Opinions of the Greater Philosophers. New York: Simon & Schuster.

Eldredge, John. (2011). Wild at Heart Revised and Updated: Discovering the Secret of a Man's Soul. Nashville: Thomas Nelson.

Missler, Chuck. (2001, November). The Gospel in Quadraphonic: Why Are There Four Gospels? Retrieved from http://khouse.org/articles/2001/378/

Morris, John D. Has Archaeological Evidence for Jesus Been Discovered? Retrieved from http://www.icr.org/article/has-archaeological-evidence-for-jesus-been-discove/

Mykytiuk, Lawrence. (2016, December 3). Did Jesus Exist? Searching for Evidence Beyond the Bible. Retrieved from http://www.biblicalarchaeology.org/daily/people-cultures-in-the-bible/jesus-historical-jesus/did-jesus-exist/

What are the different Jewish festivals in the Bible? Retrieved from https://www.gotquestions.org/Jewish-festivals.html

89218520R00059

Made in the USA
Columbia, SC
19 February 2018